# My Pain,

*My Pain, My Story, My Journey...My Life*

Living with intention, love and accountability.

By Ericka McDole

## Table of Contents

Chapter 1: The Breaking Point

Chapter 2: When They Didn't Believe Me

Chapter 3: A Life Interrupted

Chapter 4: A Love Without Permission

Chapter 5: Collateral Damage

Chapter 6: Stripped But Not Covered

Chapter 7: My Mirror Moments

Chapter 8: Rebuilding My Name

Chapter 9: The Real Me, Affirmation Revised

Chapter 10: Power Now

Chapter 11: Love Wins in the End

# My Pain, My Power

*My Pain, My Story, My Journey...My Life*

Living with intention, love and accountability.

By Ericka McDole

## Dedication

This book is dedicated to every woman who has ever been labeled too emotional, too strong, too broken, too much.

To the ones who carry their families, wear their pain like armor, and keep showing up even when they're falling apart, this is for you.

To my children, who gave me reasons to keep fighting even when I wanted to give up, thank you for your love, your grace, and your patience.

To my grandchildren, may you always know your worth, your voice, and your power.

To my husband, who has walked with me through darkness and chosen redemption over regret, this story is ours too.

To the girl I used to be, you survived, you rose, and you turned pain into power.

# My Pain, My Power

## *My Pain, My Story, My Journey...My Life*

*Living with intention, love and accountability.*

*By Ericka McDole*

And finally, to every silent survivor:
May this book be the reminder that your story matters, your voice deserves to be heard, and your healing is your birthright.

With love and gratitude,
Ericka

# My Pain, My Power

## *My Pain, My Story, My Journey...My Life*

Living with intention, love and accountability.

By Ericka McDole

## Foreword

There are stories we tell the world, and then there are stories we whisper only to ourselves. This memoir is the latter, finally spoken aloud.

Ericka McDole invites us into the sacred, unfiltered corners of her life with a bravery that both stirs and stuns. Her words do not ask for pity; they demand presence. She doesn't just recount her pain, she dissects it, examines it, and transforms it into power.

What you'll find in these pages is not a chronicle of survival, but a celebration of transformation. Ericka's journey reminds us that healing is not linear. That sometimes the strongest thing a woman can do is fall apart and rebuild herself brick by brick, tear by tear.

She doesn't sugarcoat. She doesn't mask. She stands. And in her standing, she gives permission to every reader to do the same.

# My Pain, My Power

## *My Pain, My Story, My Journey...My Life*

*Living with intention, love and accountability.*

*By Ericka McDole*

You will cry with her. You will rage beside her. You will cheer her on as she reclaims her name, her voice, and her power.

This book is not just for those who've endured betrayal, incarceration, or trauma. It's for every person who has ever had to rise from their own ruins and build again.

Thank you, Ericka, for your truth. Thank you for showing us that even the darkest chapters can end in light.

Now turn the page. The story begins.

**"She found healing not in forgetting, but finally telling truth."**

# My Pain, My Power

## *My Pain, My Story, My Journey...My Life*

Living with intention, love and accountability.

By Ericka McDole

## Acknowledgments

Writing this book was both one of the hardest and most healing things I've ever done, and I didn't do it alone.

To God, the ultimate author of my story, thank you for grace, mercy, and the strength to keep going when I felt like giving up. Thank you for never letting go, even when I did.

To my husband, thank you for choosing accountability, for choosing truth, and most importantly, for choosing us. Your growth and your willingness to do the work made space for reconciliation. I honor our journey and where we are now.

To my children, you are my heart. Thank you for your love, your understanding, and your presence through every season of my life. You are the reason I kept going.

# My Pain, My Power

## *My Pain, My Story, My Journey...My Life*

*Living with intention, love and accountability.*

*By Ericka McDole*

To my grandchildren, who are too young to fully understand this story yet, I hope one day it helps you see the strength and resilience you come from.

To my family and friends who stood by me, supported me, and never judged me, your love held me up when I couldn't hold myself.

To the women who poured into me during the darkest moments, especially those who prayed for me, cried with me, and spoke life into me, thank you for your light.

To the women I met during my short incarceration, you reminded me that compassion lives in the most unexpected places. Some of you are still in my life today, and I carry your stories with me.

To every therapist, counselor, and group facilitator who helped me do the hard work of

# My Pain, My Power

### *My Pain, My Story, My Journey...My Life*

*Living with intention, love and accountability.*

*By Ericka McDole*

healing, thank you for giving me tools I'll carry for the rest of my life.

And to every woman who picks up this book, thank you for holding space for my truth. I pray that in these pages, you find pieces of your own healing too.

With deepest gratitude,
Ericka

# My Pain, My Power

***My Pain, My Story, My Journey...My Life***

*Living with intention, love and accountability.*

*By Ericka McDole*

## About the Author

Ericka McDole, also known as Goldie, Big E, or E Money, is a devoted wife, a proud mother of three, a loving bonus mom, and a grandmother of seven. Born and raised in Saginaw, Michigan, Ericka is a licensed barber, a cycle-breaker, and a woman of deep faith and resilience.

Her journey has been anything but easy, from betrayal and a short incarceration to mental health struggles and personal transformation. Yet through it all, Ericka has still been committed to her healing, her truth, and her purpose.

A God-fearing woman, Ericka believes in living with intention, love, and accountability. Her life's work is a testament to the power of self-reflection, emotional maturity, integrity, and forgiveness, not just for others, but for herself.

This memoir is her offering to every woman who has ever been silenced, shamed, or

# My Pain, My Power

## My Pain, My Story, My Journey…My Life

Living with intention, love and accountability.

By Ericka McDole

misunderstood. It is a love letter to those who are still learning to rise from the wreckage and stand in their power.

Ericka's superpower is discernment and problem-solving, and her voice carries a message of healing for generations to come.

Connect with her, learn from her, and be reminded through her journey that even the most broken chapters can lead to the most beautiful endings.

# My Pain, My Power

## *My Pain, My Story, My Journey...My Life*

*Living with intention, love and accountability.*

*By Ericka McDole*

### Chapter 1: The Breaking Point

To every woman who has ever been labeled crazy when she was just really in pain, this is for you.

To the ones who smiled through the weight of betrayal, laughed to hide the rage, and showed up strong when they were falling apart inside, this is your story too. Welcome. Thank you for holding space here with me. I don't take it lightly.

This book is my truth. My journey. The story behind the face people think they know, the version of me that will never make it to Facebook. It's what happens when trauma meets survival, and when survival starts asking for more.

# My Pain, My Power

### *My Pain, My Story, My Journey…My Life*

*Living with intention, love and accountability.*

*By Ericka McDole*

People see the smile. They see the strength. They see the attitude I wear like armor. But they've never seen the scars. They have no idea about the nights I cried myself to sleep, the days I couldn't get out of bed, or the moments I wanted to disappear. Some people judge me without knowing half of what I've endured. They write their versions of my story without even knowing mine.

Well, this is mine.

**"They broke her open, but all they did was free the woman she was always meant to be"**

# My Pain, My Power

## *My Pain, My Story, My Journey...My Life*

*Living with intention, love and accountability.*

*By Ericka McDole*

There comes a moment in your life where you look around and no longer recognize the life you're living, or the person you've become. That was my breaking point.

It wasn't just one single moment that broke me. It was years of small fractures: the childhood pain I tucked away, the betrayal I tried to rationalize, the lies I accepted just to keep the peace, the silence I lived in just to keep others comfortable. But silence doesn't heal you. Then one day I realized I wasn't living, I was performing. And the performance was slowly killing me.

That was the moment I knew something had to change. I didn't want to live another day angry, numb, or bitter, I didn't want to be known as just the woman who survived.

# My Pain, My Power

### *My Pain, My Story, My Journey...My Life*

*Living with intention, love and accountability.*

*By Ericka McDole*

I didn't want to be known as the woman who was "so strong" and "had it all together" when I was literally breaking inside.

But I did want to be the woman who healed.

I was born in Saginaw, Michigan, a place that shaped me in ways I didn't fully understand until years later. I'm a wife, a mother of three, with a bonus child I love as my own. A grandmother of seven. A licensed barber. A manager. A leader. A cycle breaker. For so long, these were the titles I introduced myself with. But those titles didn't tell the full story.

I am not what happened to me. I am not the product of pain; I am the product of resilience. I am not crazy.

It took me years to understand that healing is not linear. There are days, I am good. Other days, I am a wreck. But the fact that I am still standing means something. The fact that I am

# My Pain, My Power

## *My Pain, My Story, My Journey...My Life*

*Living with intention, love and accountability.*

*By Ericka McDole*

showing up, even broken, means everything.

I had been strong for everyone else, my family, my children, my marriage. But I hadn't been strong for myself. I had experienced the kind of heartbreak that shatters your identity. **Infidelity** that stripped me bare. I tried to forgive, to understand, to make peace. But I never allowed myself to truly grieve. Until I did.

I was diagnosed with severe depression and anxiety. And when the pain became too heavy to carry in silence, I broke. That breaking point landed me in a jail not just once, but almost twice. A space where I was forced to sit still and confront everything I had been running from.

But jail didn't confine me, it freed me.

It was there that I began to strip away the lies I told myself to keep surviving. I began to see

# My Pain, My Power

## *My Pain, My Story, My Journey...My Life*

Living with intention, love and accountability.

By Ericka McDole

the woman beneath the pain. The woman who was still alive, still breathing, still worthy.

I had been in therapy for years, but nothing transformed me like the Intensive Outpatient Program I later attended. Those four-hour sessions broke me open. I cried. I journaled. I saw myself, fully, for the first time in a long time.

This chapter isn't about shame. It's about truth. It's the part of my story where everything fell apart so I could finally start to rebuild.

This is the beginning of my power.

# My Pain, My Power

*My Pain, My Story, My Journey...My Life*

*Living with intention, love and accountability.*

*By Ericka McDole*

## The Breaking Point

She smiled through the storm, but her hands were trembling,
Taught to hold it all in, even as the walls were crumbling.
The world saw strength, fierce and unshaken,
But they never knew the pieces, silently breaking.

She wore survival like a second skin,
A mask of "I'm fine" stretched too thin.
But silence screamed in the corners of her soul,
And her heart whispered, "This isn't whole."

There came a moment, not loud but clear,
When numbness gave way to one final tear.
No longer pretending, no more disguise,
She met her reflection and saw tired eyes.

That was the breaking, not of weakness but truth,

# My Pain, My Power

*My Pain, My Story, My Journey…My Life*

Living with intention, love and accountability.

By Ericka McDole

**The shedding of roles, the return to her youth.
No longer performing, she stood in her pain,
And from the ashes, she rose again.**

**This is where power begins, not in might
But in choosing herself in the dead of night.
Let them call it broken, but she knows it's art
The masterpiece born of a fractured heart.**

# My Pain, My Power

***My Pain, My Story, My Journey...My Life***

*Living with intention, love and accountability.*

*By Ericka McDole*

## Chapter 2: When They Didn't Believe Me

I used to think bruises had to be purple or swollen to count, that the pain had to be visible to be valid. But emotional wounds? They don't show up on skin. In fact, the deepest wounds rarely make a sound.

They show up in the way you flinch at certain words, the way you overthink every interaction, the way you apologize just for existing. They show up in distrust, perfectionism, and in always trying to prove your worth. I carried these wounds even when I didn't recognize them.

There were days I felt nothing, numb and disconnected. There were days when every nerve was on fire. The smallest thing would break me: a comment, a tone, a look. That's how trauma works. It doesn't always knock. Sometimes it sneaks in through the back door and settles in like it owns the place.

# My Pain, My Power

**My Pain, My Story, My Journey...My Life**

*Living with intention, love and accountability.*

*By Ericka McDole*

I had been angry for a long time, at myself, at God, at anyone who felt too safe to blame. I didn't understand why I had to go through so

much. Why me? Why this life? Why this pain? And then, I realized something. I wasn't cursed. I was chosen. Not chosen to suffer, but chosen to overcome, to heal, to teach, to be a living example of what resilience looks like. But healing meant confronting the parts of me I had buried deep, the parts that were still bleeding.

It meant breaking down to break through.

My childhood memories are a collage of contradictions. There were laughs and lessons, but also silence and shame. My home was a game of emotional hopscotch. I learned how to read the room before I knew how to spell my name. I was forced to grow up fast. Too fast.

No one warns a little girl that trust can be snatched in a single moment. That once it's gone,

# My Pain, My Power

## *My Pain, My Story, My Journey...My Life*

*Living with intention, love and accountability.*

*By Ericka McDole*

everything else feels like a test. I learned early that trust is not a given, it's a privilege. And if I couldn't count on anyone else, I could count on myself.
My survival mode had no on-and-off switch. I stayed on edge, always ready for the next challenge. They say, it looked like I had an attitude. Like I was problematic, stubborn, or "grown." But inside, it was pure fight-or-flight, pumping through my veins long before I understood what adrenaline was.

People praised my survival mode like it was a badge of honor. "You're so strong." They didn't know the cost. They didn't know how my jaw never unclenched. How silence felt suspicious, and kindness felt calculated. Years later, a therapist gave it a name: **hypervigilance**. I only knew it as normal.

I got straight A's in survival. But it cost me everything.

# My Pain, My Power

## *My Pain, My Story, My Journey...My Life*

*Living with intention, love and accountability.*

*By Ericka McDole*

I left home early. I became a mother early. I never asked for help because neediness had always been punished. Self-sufficiency felt safer than love. Vulnerability wasn't an option, it was a liability.

One day in sixth grade, I told a counselor at school about some things that were happening to me. I didn't know about mandatory reporting. I thought I was talking to someone I could trust. Someone who cared.

But after that conversation, everything changed.

There wasn't physical abuse, but the tension was thick. It was always, "You better get her." I felt silenced. I felt blamed. I didn't know it then, but it was the beginning of being seen as a problem. A deviant. A girl who didn't know her place.

And if you're reading this, and you were one of the people who didn't believe me, I forgive you. But I still must speak my truth. Because this is

# My Pain, My Power

## *My Pain, My Story, My Journey...My Life*

*Living with intention, love and accountability.*

*By Ericka McDole*

my healing.

The damage did not just affect me, it bled into my relationships. Into my marriage. Into my parenting. Into my peace. It took me nearly 40 years to let go of the resentment I carried. I had to stop waiting for the apology I never received and start healing for me.

I'm not excusing what happened. I'm not pretending it didn't matter. But I chose to not let it define me. Holding on to that pain only continued the damage, not just to my heart, but to everything I touched.

And one of the greatest lessons I learned? Believe children. Listen without judgment. Don't minimize someone's pain just because it's hard to hear. Don't sweep it under the rug.

This is part of my story. The part I didn't get to tell, until now.

# My Pain, My Power

## *My Pain, My Story, My Journey...My Life*

*Living with intention, love and accountability.*

*By Ericka McDole*

This chapter is for the ones whose pain wasn't seen. For the girls who were called grown when they were just hurting. For the women still carrying scars no one ever noticed.

You don't need permission to speak your truth.

This is mine.

**"They questioned my story but can't silence my truth. My truth still stands, even if I had to stand in it alone"**

# My Pain, My Power

*My Pain, My Story, My Journey...My Life*

Living with intention, love and accountability.

By Ericka McDole

## When They Did Not Believe Me

I spoke with a trembling voice they chose not to hear,
My truth dismissed, replaced with fear.
Not fists, but silence, cut the deepest slice,
When your pain is doubted, you pay the price.

I wore wounds that didn't show on skin,
Battles raging silently within.
Told to hush, to shrink, to behave,
While my spirit tried its best to be brave.

The labels came quickly "too much," "too wild,"
But no one remembered I was just a child.
A heart still forming, already bruised,
Punished for pain I didn't choose.

But I kept breathing, even though blame,
Refused to carry someone else's shame.

# My Pain, My Power

## *My Pain, My Story, My Journey...My Life*

*Living with intention, love and accountability.*

*By Ericka McDole*

And now I speak, not for pity, but peace,
To release the weight, to find my release.

So, if you hear my voice and it shakes,
Know it's from all the times it broke and remade.
I believe me. And that's enough.
My truth stands firm, even when it's tough.

# My Pain, My Power

### *My Pain, My Story, My Journey...My Life*

*Living with intention, love and accountability.*

*By Ericka McDole*

## Chapter 3: A Life Interrupted

There are moments in life that split you in two, the person you were before, and the person you become after. This was one of those moments.

This chapter isn't just about betrayal. It's about what happens when love, the kind you pour your soul into, shatters your heart so violently that you're left piecing yourself together through tears and prayers. When love breaks you, but doesn't destroy you, it teaches you who you are beneath the weight of survival.

I loved my husband. Fully, deeply, and with a loyalty that didn't waiver even when things were hard. We'd been together since we were kids. I was his backbone. I prayed for him, supported him, covered him in every way I knew how. And for a while, I believed that kind of love would be enough to protect us. But it wasn't.

# My Pain, My Power

## *My Pain, My Story, My Journey...My Life*

Living with intention, love and accountability.

By Ericka McDole

Infidelity crept in like poison. Quiet at first, then all-consuming. And when the truth came out, that he had child on the way with someone else, it felt like the ground gave way beneath my feet.

I made the choice to accept the child. Not because I had to, but because I chose love. I believed in redemption. I believed in trying. I believed in family. And I believed that if I showed grace, maybe the pain wouldn't swallow me whole.

But then came the real heartbreak, the part no one warns you about. The part where the woman who slept with your husband enters your life and starts rewriting your story. She didn't just have a baby, she brought **war**. She created **chaos**. She positioned herself in my world like she belonged there, like she had a right to stand where I stood. And somehow, in her mind, I was the problem.

She wasn't content with her role, she wanted mine. And when she couldn't have it, she did

# My Pain, My Power

## *My Pain, My Story, My Journey...My Life*

*Living with intention, love and accountability.*

*By Ericka McDole*

what broken people often do: she projected. She despised me. Not because I wronged her. Not because I lied to her. But because I was what she would never be, I was **the wife**. I was the one he committed to. I was the life she fantasized about but could never truly have.

One of the most devastating consequences of this betrayal wasn't just emotional. It was physical. Tangible. It cost me my freedom.

I ended up in jail, yes, jail, because of the chaos she brought into my life, I snapped. And while I won't disclose every detail, know this: I don't regret what I did but, I went to jail behind someone who was never supposed to be part of my journey. I didn't break into her life; she broke into mine, and what happened she deserved.

But I was the one who was punished. I was the one torn from my children. From my home. From

# My Pain, My Power

## *My Pain, My Story, My Journey...My Life*

*Living with intention, love and accountability.*

*By Ericka McDole*

the very life I was trying to hold together. That separation, that humiliation, left wounds deeper than any betrayal.

But let me be clear about something, through it all, I was never alone. My family knew my heart. My friends knew my character. The people who mattered stood beside me, because they had seen the love, the sacrifice, and the strength I had always given.

She didn't lie on me. She didn't need to. She lived in a fantasy that tried to replace my reality. But fantasy has no roots in truth. And truth, my truth, has always stood firm.

There were days when I thought the pain would consume me. When I couldn't eat. When I couldn't breathe without crying. When I would go into a room and collapse on the floor just to feel something other than the weight of betrayal.

# My Pain, My Power

## My Pain, My Story, My Journey...My Life

*Living with intention, love and accountability.*

*By Ericka McDole*

But I didn't stay there.
I wrote affirmations on mirrors just to remind myself that I existed outside of this pain. That I mattered. That I was still whole even if everything around me was broken.

This chapter is for the woman who tried to do everything right and still got shattered. For the wife who held it down, only to watch someone else play pretend with her life. For the mother who had to be strong even when she was crumbling.

You may be interrupted, but you are not erased.

I am not the same woman I was before this storm. I am stronger. Wiser. Louder. I don't shrink for anyone, not anymore.

Let them think what they want. Let her keep chasing shadows. I live in the light now.
And I will never again apologize for surviving what was meant to destroy me.

# My Pain, My Power

## My Pain, My Story, My Journey…My Life

Living with intention, love and accountability.

By Ericka McDole

"I was his backbone until betrayal bent me in half. But I stand again, because my worth was never tied to someone else's delusion."

# My Pain, My Power

*My Pain, My Story, My Journey...My Life*

*Living with intention, love and accountability.*

*By Ericka McDole*

### A Life Interrupted

**You shattered me, not with fists,**

**But with secrets sealed in lips once kissed.**

**A love I gave without condition,**

**Turned into war without permission.**

**I held him up through every storm,**

**Believed that faith would keep us warm.**

**But even strong hearts crack and bleed,**

**When trust is traded for selfish need.**

**She came like thunder in disguise,**

**With a baby, but also lies.**

**Not lies told aloud or heard,**

# My Pain, My Power

*My Pain, My Story, My Journey...My Life*

Living with intention, love and accountability.

By Ericka McDole

But lived through chaos, cold and blurred.

She didn't need to break my name,

Just played a part in a losing game.

Not a villain in the eyes of many,

But to her, I was too much of plenty.

The wife, the mother, the home, the grace,

She tried to steal but couldn't replace.

Because you can wear the role for show,

But roots don't grow where lies still flow.

They took my peace, they took my breath,

Even sent me to jail like a slow death.

But freedoms not found behind locked doors

It's found in choosing what you restore.

# My Pain, My Power

*My Pain, My Story, My Journey…My Life*

*Living with intention, love and accountability.*

*By Ericka McDole*

I returned from that dark, cold place,

With jagged pieces, but steady grace.

Wrote on mirrors to remind my soul,

That I am broken, but still whole.

So, this is for the ones who ache,

Who gave and watched their world break.

We are not ruined, not erased

We're just reborn in softer space.

Let them gossip, let them doubt,

I've cried my truth and purged it out.

This life was mine before her games

And I rise again without the shame.

# My Pain, My Power

## *My Pain, My Story, My Journey...My Life*

*Living with intention, love and accountability.*

*By Ericka McDole*

"Some loves are born form chaos not from choice. And sometimes the bravest thing a woman can do is love what came from the deepest hurt, without needing permission to do so."

# My Pain, My Power

## *My Pain, My Story, My Journey...My Life*

*Living with intention, love and accountability.*

*By Ericka McDole*

### Chapter 4: A Love Without Permission

The day my husband brought her home, she was only a month old. A baby, innocent, soft, unaware of the storm she was born into.

I didn't know how I was supposed to feel. How do you hold the child that came from your husband's betrayal? How do you love through that kind of pain? But I did. I held her. I looked at her. And I made a choice that day, not for him, not for her mother, but for me.

I chose love.

I didn't want that baby to carry the burden of her parents' decisions. I didn't want her to feel like a mistake, like a reminder of destruction. I wanted her to know peace, to grow up in truth, to have a relationship with her siblings that wasn't tainted by resentment or shame.

# My Pain, My Power

## My Pain, My Story, My Journey...My Life

*Living with intention, love and accountability.*

By Ericka McDole

I tried to co-parent with her mother. I tried because I believed that maybe, just maybe, we could make the best of a bad situation. That two grown women could set aside their feelings and show a little girl what maturity, grace, and accountability looked like.

I knew the child was innocent. She didn't ask for this. And so, I tried to replace the pain I felt with love. I tried to mother from a place of healing, even though I was still hurting. I showed up for her, because it was the right thing to do.

But that didn't work for her mother.

She didn't want peace. She didn't want grace. She didn't want forgiveness.

She wanted my husband.

No matter how much I tried to bridge the gap, she lit it on fire. It was never about co-parenting.

# My Pain, My Power

## My Pain, My Story, My Journey...My Life

*Living with intention, love and accountability.*

By Ericka McDole

It was never about the child. It was about control. About fantasy. About trying to take my place. But a position in someone's life doesn't mean you've earned a place in their heart.

She wanted what I had, but she didn't want the responsibility that came with it. She wanted the love, the title, the home. But she didn't want the truth, the work, or the growth.

And while she played a game of control, I was still trying to create peace. For that child. For my children. For myself.

I had to look at a baby born from betrayal and still offer her love, protection, and connection. I had to quiet the screams in my soul and show up as more than a wounded wife. I had to be a woman of faith, of grace, of strength, even when I was falling apart.

Because the child was never the problem. The child was never my enemy. And I refused to let

# My Pain, My Power

## *My Pain, My Story, My Journey...My Life*

*Living with intention, love and accountability.*

*By Ericka McDole*

her carry the weight of decisions that were never hers to make.

This chapter is not about blame, it's about choice. And I chose love. Even when it hurt. Even when it wasn't returned. Even when it was met with resistance and manipulation.

That child may never know the depth of what I sacrificed to create peace for her. But I know. God knows.

And that's enough.

**"She may never understand the cost of the love I gave, but I do. I chose peace when I had every reason not to, and that will always be my power."**

# My Pain, My Power

## *My Pain, My Story, My Journey...My Life*

*Living with intention, love and accountability.*

*By Ericka McDole*

### A Love Without Permission

**She came wrapped in silence, just a month old,**

**A child born into storms I never asked to hold.**

**She was not the betrayal, she was its echo,**

**Yet I looked in her eyes and let my love flow.**

**I held her with trembling hands,**

**Wrestling truth no one understands.**

**How do you mother through heartbreak's fire?**

**How do you choose peace over vengeance and ire?**

**I did not choose the wound,**

**But I chose not to bleed on her soul.**

**She was innocence, untouched by lies,**

# My Pain, My Power

## *My Pain, My Story, My Journey...My Life*

Living with intention, love and accountability.

By Ericka McDole

**And so, I fought to make her whole.**

**I tried to build bridges from grace,**

**To co-parent in a sacred space.**

**Not for the one who sought to take,**

**But for the child who didn't make the mistake.**

**Her mother wanted more than repair,**

**She wanted the throne, the crown, the air.**

**She played house in a fantasy game,**

**But love without truth only burns in shame.**

**I gave what I didn't have to spare,**

**A quiet strength wrapped in prayer.**

**She may never know what it cost me to stay,**

**To smile while grief took pieces away.**

**But heaven saw, and God took note,**

# My Pain, My Power

## *My Pain, My Story, My Journey...My Life*

*Living with intention, love and accountability.*

*By Ericka McDole*

Of every tear I didn't quote.

This wasn't surrender, it was sacred war,

A woman choosing love when she could've closed the door.

So, this poem is for that silent choice,

For every time I silenced my voice,

To give a child what she deserved to see.

# My Pain, My Power

### *My Pain, My Story, My Journey...My Life*

*Living with intention, love and accountability.*

*By Ericka McDole*

## Chapter 5: Collateral Damage

One of the most devastating consequences of my husband's infidelity wasn't just the

betrayal. It wasn't just the child that was born from it. It was what that betrayal cost

me, emotionally, mentally, spiritually… and eventually, physically.

It cost me my freedom.

I went to jail. Yes, jail. And I'm not ashamed to say that anymore, because if you only knew

the weight I was carrying, the battles I had fought silently, the lies I had swallowed just to

keep peace… you might understand how a woman like me, who kept showing up, finally

snapped.

# My Pain, My Power

## My Pain, My Story, My Journey...My Life

Living with intention, love and accountability.

By Ericka McDole

I didn't end up in jail because I was out of control. I ended up there because I had been

controlled for too long. I had been pushed to my breaking point. It wasn't just the other

woman, it was the weight of years spent holding everything together while I was falling

apart inside.

The first few days were hell. I was in a holding cell with three or four other women, sleeping

on cold cement with those thin-ass mats, eating paper bag meals. One of the women had just had a baby and was still shedding from childbirth. The smell was torturous. The experience was inhumane.

Around the fourth day, I heard it: "McDole!" The door unlocked, and I was processed as an actual inmate of the Saginaw County Jail. They moved me into general population, gen pop.

# My Pain, My Power

## *My Pain, My Story, My Journey...My Life*

Living with intention, love and accountability.

By Ericka McDole

When I walked in and saw how many women were in there, I thought, "Now Lord, how is this going to work? You know I don't like being around a lot of women."

But then I looked to my left and saw a familiar face on one of the bottom bunks. What were the odds? Well, in Saginaw, maybe not so rare. But still, it shook me. It grounded me.

That first week and a half felt like an out-of-body experience. I kept wondering if I was dreaming. Having someone I knew there helped. But I was still angry. Still humiliated. Still in disbelief.

Then one day I heard it again: "McDole!" I walked to the door and the officer asked if I wanted to be a trustee. For those who don't know, a trustee lives in a different part of the jail called a dorm.

Trustees work in the kitchen, get an extra snack at night, and we even got to wear real tennis shoes from outside instead of those hard-ass jail

# My Pain, My Power

## *My Pain, My Story, My Journey…My Life*

*Living with intention, love and accountability.*

By Ericka McDole

shoes. It didn't feel like a privilege. It felt like an assignment.

Because here's the part I never expected: even in jail, people gravitated to me.

Women started calling me "Momma." They came to me for advice, for comfort, for prayer.

Even while I was hurting, I found myself pouring into others. Covering others.

Encouraging others.

That jail stripped me, but it did not take my calling.

I did not seek leadership, it found me, even behind bars. And some of those women, they still keep in touch with me to this day. They saw something in me, even when I did not see it in myself. They reminded me that even in the pit, I had purpose.

# My Pain, My Power

## *My Pain, My Story, My Journey...My Life*

Living with intention, love and accountability.

By Ericka McDole

That experience broke me, but it also revealed me.

I was collateral damage in someone else's war, but I came out of it with a deeper sense of who I am. Not just a wife. Not just a mother. But a woman of impact, even in the darkest of places.

This chapter is for the women who were judged by a single moment and not the life that led up to

it. For the women who broke because they were tired of bending. For the ones who were punished for reacting instead of being protected from the cause.

I may have been stripped. I may have been sentenced. But I was never silenced.

I walked out of that place humbled, wiser, and ready to reclaim every piece of myself they thought I would leave behind.

I was collateral damage, but I became a force.

# My Pain, My Power

## *My Pain, My Story, My Journey...My Life*

*Living with intention, love and accountability.*

*By Ericka McDole*

"I was punished for surviving what was meant to destroy me, but purpose still found me. I wasn't the cause; I was the coat. Collateral, but never defeated."

# My Pain, My Power

*My Pain, My Story, My Journey...My Life*

Living with intention, love and accountability.

By Ericka McDole

### Collateral Damage

Women gravitated toward my light,

Called me "Momma" in the middle I was pushed to the edge, where silence screams,

Where broken hearts shatter lifelong dreams.

Not by my hands, but by another's deceit,

I fell to my knees, still refusing defeat.

My children felt absence, my soul felt shame,

Yet none of this mess carried my name.

I wore the blame she tried to assign,

But my truth stood firm, it would not resign.

Bars couldn't hold what God designed,

Even behind walls, I still shined.

of night.

# My Pain, My Power

## *My Pain, My Story, My Journey...My Life*

*Living with intention, love and accountability.*

*By Ericka McDole*

They found in me what the world had missed,

A steady voice, a healing kiss.

Even there, purpose found me again,

Proving broken places still can mend.

I paid a price for a crime not mine,

But grace wrote the ending, line by line

This is the story behind the rage,

Love interrupted, pain on stage.

But I rose, not just for me,

For every woman lost at sea.

You are not what tried to erase you,

You are what God raised you through.

# My Pain, My Power

*My Pain, My Story, My Journey...My Life*

Living with intention, love and accountability.

By Ericka McDole

## Chapter 6: Stripped But Not Covered

There are moments in life when you are stripped bare, of titles, of dignity, of identity. Not physically, but emotionally. Spiritually. Internally. This was one of those moments.

After the jail cell. After the silence. After the betrayal. I was no longer who I had been. But I didn't yet know who I was becoming.

I was stripped. Not just of the illusions, but of the armor I had been wearing my entire life.

The performance I had perfected, the strong one, the capable one, the one who had it all together, was no longer sustainable. It cracked open. And when it did, I was left exposed.

Stripped, but not covered.

People often say "you're so strong" like it's a compliment. They don't see the cost of that strength. They don't see how it was built from broken pieces, held together with silent suffering

# My Pain, My Power

## *My Pain, My Story, My Journey...My Life*

*Living with intention, love and accountability.*

*By Ericka McDole*

and quiet prayers whispered in bathrooms, closets, and parked cars. They don't see the nights I laid awake feeling like a ghost in my own life.

I wasn't always strong. I just had no other choice.

And when the mask came off, I had to sit with myself. The real me. The one who was

exhausted. The one who had been giving and giving while bleeding internally. The one who had forgotten what it felt like to be nurtured, held, or poured into.

Being stripped showed me how much of myself I had given away trying to be everything for everyone else. I had become so used to performing that I didn't even recognize when the act became my identity.

But beneath the performance was a woman full of questions. Full of grief. Full of unresolved trauma that had been shoved into dark corners for years.

# My Pain, My Power

***My Pain, My Story, My Journey...My Life***

*Living with intention, love and accountability.*

*By Ericka McDole*

This was the season when I started facing the truth, not just about others, but about myself.

I had to acknowledge the ways I stayed silent when I should've spoken up. The ways I let things slide for the sake of peace. The ways I dismissed my own needs and desires just to make sure everyone else was okay.

This wasn't just about what had been done to me. It was about what I had allowed, what I had tolerated, and what I had internalized.

Self-accountability is not self-blame, it's self-liberation.

I had to learn how to forgive myself for not knowing better, for not protecting my peace more fiercely, for blaming myself for the actions of others. I had to look in the mirror, not with judgment, but with

# My Pain, My Power

## My Pain, My Story, My Journey...My Life

*Living with intention, love and accountability.*

*By Ericka McDole*

compassion.

I wasn't a failure. I was a woman in process.

This chapter is about that uncomfortable middle. The raw space between who I was and who I was becoming. The space where everything hurt, but healing had begun.

I was stripped, but not destroyed. Exposed, but not erased. And now, I was finally ready to rebuild, but this time, as my whole self.

# My Pain, My Power

*My Pain, My Story, My Journey...My Life*

*Living with intention, love and accountability.*

*By Ericka McDole*

### Stripped But Not Covered

They called me strong,

But they never saw me stripped.

Not of clothes, but of certainty,

Of the armor I so tightly gripped.

They saw the smile, not the scream,

Heard my laugh, not my plea.

I was the helper, the healer, the light,

But no one came to rescue me.

I broke in silence, behind closed doors,

Where no applause could reach.

And there I met the truest me,

Beyond the strength I tried to preach.

Stripped, but not covered.

# My Pain, My Power

## *My Pain, My Story, My Journey...My Life*

*Living with intention, love and accountability.*

*By Ericka McDole*

Exposed in all my ache.

No title, no applause, no filter,

Just the truth I could no longer fake.

I poured from an empty cup,

Until even the cup was gone.

And only then did I realize

Performing had lasted too long.

The mirror didn't lie.

It showed the woman beneath the mask,

The one who held her breath for peace,

The one afraid to ask.

I forgave her for staying too long,

For quieting her own need.

She wasn't weak, she was surviving.

# My Pain, My Power

*My Pain, My Story, My Journey…My Life*

Living with intention, love and accountability.

By Ericka McDole

She was planting healing's seed.

This poem is for the unbecoming,

For the undoing, raw and real.

The kind of broken that clears the path,

For the kind of whole that heals.

So, call me strong, but know the cost.

Know what I've had to lose.

Stripped, but still standing.

Now I finally get to choose.

# My Pain, My Power

## *My Pain, My Story, My Journey...My Life*

*Living with intention, love and accountability.*

*By Ericka McDole*

**"The world saw strength. I only knew the war it came from."**

# My Pain, My Power

***My Pain, My Story, My Journey...My Life***

*Living with intention, love and accountability.*

*By Ericka McDole*

## Chapter 7: My Mirror Moments

There comes a time when survival isn't enough. When waking up each day and simply "making it" becomes too heavy to bear. That was the season I found myself in, broken, bruised, and finally brave enough to confront my reflection.

I started putting affirmations on every mirror in my house, bathroom, bedroom, hallway, it didn't matter. Wherever I turned, I forced myself to look at words I wasn't sure I believed yet: "You are worthy." "You are not your past." "You are enough." I didn't feel it.

But I needed to see it. Every. Single. Day.

These mirror moments were more than just habit, they were lifelines. I was speaking life into myself when everything in me felt lifeless. I was battling shame with every sticky note. I was choosing truth over trauma, one word at a time. The truth is, I didn't know who I was outside of the pain. Outside of the roles I had played so

# My Pain, My Power

## *My Pain, My Story, My Journey...My Life*

*Living with intention, love and accountability.*

*By Ericka McDole*

well, the wife, the mother, the strong friend, the one who holds it down. The mirror exposed what I had been avoiding: the real me.

I realized I had spent years performing. I knew how to show up, how to smile, how to put on for the world, but deep down I was crumbling. My mirror didn't lie. It didn't filter. It made me confront the very parts of me I had been trying to hide.

That woman staring back at me was not weak, but she was weary. She was not broken, but she was bleeding. She wasn't a failure; she was just finally feeling everything she had buried.

There were days I stood in front of the mirror crying. Other days I stood silently, just

breathing, trying to exist. But slowly, word by word, day by day, I began to see her. Me. and I began to love her.

I wrote things like, "You're not crazy, you're in pain." "You deserve the same grace you give to

# My Pain, My Power

## My Pain, My Story, My Journey...My Life

Living with intention, love and accountability.

By Ericka McDole

others." "God is not done with you." And as crazy as it sounds, I started to believe it.

This was the work. Not the glamorous healing people post about online, but the private, sacred, raw kind of healing that only happens when no one's watching.

I had to take responsibility for the things I had ignored in myself. My silence. My triggers.

My lack of boundaries. My need for external validation. And I had to learn to sit with

discomfort and not run from it.

That mirror held me accountable. It challenged me. But it also embraced me. It reminded me that I didn't have to have it all figured out, I just had to be honest.

And honesty? That was the beginning of emotional maturity for me.

# My Pain, My Power

## *My Pain, My Story, My Journey...My Life*

*Living with intention, love and accountability.*

*By Ericka McDole*

I started showing up for myself the way I had always shown up for everyone else. I set boundaries. I said no. I allowed myself to rest. I cried when I needed to. I stopped

apologizing for existing.

I'm still healing. Still growing. But now when I look in the mirror, I don't just see pain. I see power.

These mirror moments taught me how to live again. How to affirm myself. How to recognize my own voice. And more than anything, how to love the woman staring back at me.

Not because she's perfect. But because she's me.

# My Pain, My Power

*My Pain, My Story, My Journey...My Life*

Living with intention, love and accountability.

By Ericka McDole

### My Mirror Moments

I stood before the mirror, tired and torn,

Not who I was, not yet reborn.

Just a woman unraveling truth from disguise,

With swollen eyes and silent cries.

Each note I placed was a whisper of hope,

A rope of words to help me cope.

You are worthy, you are enough.

Sticky truths when life was rough.

I didn't believe them, at least not yet,

But survival alone was a silent debt.

So, I spoke to my soul through paper and glass,

And found the courage to let the pain pass.

# My Pain, My Power

## *My Pain, My Story, My Journey...My Life*

*Living with intention, love and accountability.*

*By Ericka McDole*

"You are not your past," I wrote in blue,

As if seeing it might make it true.

And slowly, the tears began to say,

"You are healing, come what may."

That mirror didn't flatter or bend,

It became my counselor, my quiet friend.

It reflected not just what others see

But the woman God was calling me to be.

Some days I stared in stillness,

Some days I wept in prayer,

But every moment carved a path

Back to the woman who was always there.

She wasn't crazy, she was in pain.

She wasn't weak, she'd survived the rain.

# My Pain, My Power

*My Pain, My Story, My Journey...My Life*

Living with intention, love and accountability.

By Ericka McDole

And now she was learning to speak again.

Not for applause, but to reclaim her name.

No longer just the giver, the fixer, the wall,

She was learning she did not have to bear it all.

She set boundaries, she said "no."

And learned it's brave to let brokenness show.

This poem is for the mirror gaze,

The brave reflection in the haze.

For the woman rebuilding soul by soul,

Who found her truth and took back control.

I see you now, through glass and grace.

Not the mask, but the sacred face.

Not just the wounds, but the light within

# My Pain, My Power

## My Pain, My Story, My Journey...My Life

*Living with intention, love and accountability.*

*By Ericka McDole*

**And I love her, again and again.**

"I met myself in the mirror, not the version the world wanted, but the one who survived it all. And for the first time in a long time, I didn't look away. I looked deeper, and I love her."

# My Pain, My Power

*My Pain, My Story, My Journey...My Life*

Living with intention, love and accountability.

By Ericka McDole

## Chapter 8: Rebuilding My Name, Power

Rebuilding is not as simple as starting over, it's tearing down what no longer serves you, brick by brick, while finding the courage to believe that you deserve more. It's messy. It is lonely. It is sacred. And it's exactly what I had to do.

There comes a moment when you stop trying to fix what's broken and start rebuilding. something new. That was my choice, not just to survive what happened to me, but to transform it. I had to start by taking accountability, not for what was done to me, but for how I showed up in my pain. I had to own my silence, my people-pleasing, my tendency to pour from an empty cup, and my unwillingness to set boundaries because I feared being seen as selfish. I had to stop waiting for apologies that were never coming, and instead begin forgiving myself for tolerating what I should've walked away from.

# My Pain, My Power

## My Pain, My Story, My Journey...My Life

*Living with intention, love and accountability.*

By Ericka McDole

Accountability doesn't mean self-blame. It means reclaiming your power. It means being so rooted in integrity that no one can twist your truth.

I began to understand that forgiveness, real forgiveness, is not for them. It's for you. It's not approval of their actions, it's freedom from their grip. I did not want to walk around with

a heart hardened by resentment. I didn't want my kids to inherit my bitterness. I wanted peace more than I wanted revenge.

Forgiveness became a choice I made daily, sometimes hourly. Not because they deserved it, but because I did.

Therapy helped me start that process. But it wasn't until I entered the Intensive Outpatient Program (IOP) that everything started to shift. That program broke something in me that needed to be broken. It pulled the curtain back on my patterns, my trauma responses, my deep-rooted fears.

# My Pain, My Power

## My Pain, My Story, My Journey...My Life

*Living with intention, love and accountability.*

*By Ericka McDole*

Every day for weeks, Monday through Friday, 9 a.m. to 1 p.m., I was in group sessions, individual reflection, journaling, crying, sometimes in silence, sometimes uncontrollably. I found out things about myself that I didn't even know were hiding.

I had been in therapy for years, but IOP hit different. It forced me to sit still. To listen. To speak. To hear my own voice trembling with truth and still keep going. There's something raw about telling your story in front of strangers and being met with nods instead of judgment. With "me too" instead of silence.

I learned emotional maturity. That healing isn't linear. That some days I would be strong, and other days I'd be wrecked. But showing up, even broken, was still powerful.

Rebuilding my name meant letting go of the version of me who only lived for others'.

# My Pain, My Power

## *My Pain, My Story, My Journey...My Life*

*Living with intention, love and accountability.*

*By Ericka McDole*

approval. Rebuilding my power meant making peace with the past, even the chapters that hurt to read. Rebuilding meant finally seeing myself as worthy, without the title, without the role, without the mask.

I am not what happened to me.

I am not just the wife who stayed. I am not the one who broke or the one who rebuilt. I am both. I am layered. I am evolving.

This is what reclaiming your name looks like. Not waiting for the world to validate you, but standing tall in your own truth, your own healing, your own power.

Now.

Because I did not come this far just to survive. I came to rise. To rebuild. To reclaim.

And this, this is only the beginning.

# My Pain, My Power

*My Pain, My Story, My Journey...My Life*

Living with intention, love and accountability.

By Ericka McDole

### Rebuilding My Name

I built my name from broken stone,

Each scar a brick I call my own.

I didn't rise with polished grace,

But with trembling hands and a tear-stained face.

This wasn't healing on display,

It was whispered truth and dark dismay.

Forgiveness not for show or fame,

But a soft rebellion in my name.

I peeled back silence, shame, and fear,

Faced the lies I used to hold dear.

Not to blame, but to reclaim,

The sacred power behind my name.

# My Pain, My Power

*My Pain, My Story, My Journey...My Life*

Living with intention, love and accountability.

By Ericka McDole

I stopped waiting for "I'm sorry" sounds,

And stitched my worth from deeper grounds.

No title earned, no mask retained,

Just raw soul, unapologetically named.

Therapy gave me space to feel,

But IOP made the fracture real.

I cried in circles, journaled pain,

Watched my storms become my rain.

Emotional truths, I faced them whole,

The cost of peace, the weight of soul.

Some days brave, some days torn,

But each one proof I was reborn.

I wrote my power in quiet lines.

Refused to shrink, refused to mime.

# My Pain, My Power

## *My Pain, My Story, My Journey...My Life*

*Living with intention, love and accountability.*

*By Ericka McDole*

This woman now? She lives out loud,

Unafraid, unmasked, proud.

So, say my name with reverence now,

It carries grace and grit somehow.

I didn't just survive the flame,

I rose rebuilt; I rose renamed.

"They tried to define me by the damage, but I wrote my name in healing. And this time, I'm the one holding the pen."

# My Pain, My Power

*My Pain, My Story, My Journey...My Life*

Living with intention, love and accountability.

By Ericka McDole

## Chapter 9: The Real Me, Affirmation Revised

There was a time when I did not know who I was unless I was needed by someone else.

For years, I let the world define me by what I did for others. The support I gave. The strength I showed. The way I kept pushing, kept holding on, kept showing up. But when the storm finally settled, when the house was quiet, the kids grown, the marriage scarred but still standing, I had to ask myself: who am I when no one is watching?

I had lived so long through the lens of obligation and performance that I didn't recognize the real me beneath the layers. And I couldn't find her until I started rewriting the way I spoke to myself.

That's when I returned to the mirror.

# My Pain, My Power

## *My Pain, My Story, My Journey…My Life*

Living with intention, love and accountability.

By Ericka McDole

Not the version of me that needed validation, but the version that needed truth. I stood in front of those mirrors and spoke new affirmations, not just pretty phrases, but declarations soaked in honesty and intention.

"I forgive you."

"You're not responsible for their healing."

"You are safe now."

"You don't have to perform anymore."

Each morning, I added more. Some came through tears. Others came through whispers when my voice felt too shaky to speak them aloud. But I said them anyway. And slowly, the real me started to show up.

She was not perfect, but she was present.

She was not fearless, but she was brave enough to stay.

# My Pain, My Power

### *My Pain, My Story, My Journey...My Life*

*Living with intention, love and accountability.*

By Ericka McDole

She was not whole yet, but she was healing, and that was enough.

I began to understand that affirmation is more than self-talk, it's self-honoring. It is choosing to speak life even when death is familiar. It's meeting your reflection with grace instead of criticism. It's daring to believe that despite what happened, despite who left, despite what was lost... you are still worthy.

The real me doesn't beg for love anymore. She gives it to herself freely. The real me doesn't shrink to fit anymore. She takes up space without apology. The real me doesn't keep bleeding for people who never brought her a bandage.

She doesn't chase closure. She creates peace.

This chapter of my life is not about becoming someone new; it's about finally returning to myself.

# My Pain, My Power

## *My Pain, My Story, My Journey...My Life*

*Living with intention, love and accountability.*

*By Ericka McDole*

The real me is complex. She's been through war, but she walks with softness. She has been mislabeled, misunderstood, and mishandled, but she's still here.

She is not defined by her mistakes. She is defined by her comeback.

This is my affirmation, revised: I am not broken, I am breaking through.

I am not what they did to me, I am what I choose to become.

And I choose me.

**"They couldn't carry my depth, so they tried to diminish it. But I rose, whole, wise and unbothered, gathering strength they never prepared to face."**

# My Pain, My Power

## *My Pain, My Story, My Journey...My Life*

*Living with intention, love and accountability.*

*By Ericka McDole*

### The Real Me, Affirmation Revised

She used to answer to silence,

To sacrifice dressed as strength,

To a name whispered only when needed

But no more.

She found herself in the stillness,

In the quiet that once felt like loss,

In the words she placed on mirrors,

When her soul forgot how to speak.

No longer a vessel for everyone else's healing,

She poured truth into her own reflection.

"I forgive you," she whispered,

And it echoed through her bones.

She rose, tired, tender, whole in pieces.

# My Pain, My Power

***My Pain, My Story, My Journey...My Life***

*Living with intention, love and accountability.*

*By Ericka McDole*

Not to be seen, but to finally see herself.

No cape. No mask. Just presence.

Just breath. Just being.

The real her did not ask for permission.

She entered the room with purpose,

Took up space with grace,

And loved herself without apology.

No more begging for bare-minimum love.

No more performing pain behind strength.

She became her own soft landing,

Her own safe place to land.

They did not break her,

They broke the illusion.

And what remained was sacred:

# My Pain, My Power

*My Pain, My Story, My Journey...My Life*

*Living with intention, love and accountability.*

By Ericka McDole

A woman no longer waiting to be chosen.

She chose herself,

Every scar, every whisper, every truth.

This is not rebirth.

This is homecoming.

She is not broken,

She is breakthrough.

She is not the echo,

She is the voice.

And in every mirror now,

She sees not just survival,

But power, peace, and poetry

Written in her own name.

# My Pain, My Power

***My Pain, My Story, My Journey...My Life***

Living with intention, love and accountability.

By Ericka McDole

## Chapter 10: Power Now

Power is not always loud. It does not always look like winning. Sometimes it's getting out of

bed when your soul feels heavy. Sometimes it's choosing not to respond, walking away, or simply breathing when all you want to do is scream.

Power is what I reclaimed the moment I stopped waiting for someone to save me and decided to save myself.

For years, I was a woman who adapted to chaos. Who mistook pain for purpose. Who thought strength meant never falling apart. But healing taught me otherwise. It taught me that vulnerability is not weakness, it's courage in its purest form.

And now, I live in that courage.

I stopped living for the version of me that needed to be strong for everyone else. Now, I choose to

# My Pain, My Power

## My Pain, My Story, My Journey...My Life

*Living with intention, love and accountability.*

By Ericka McDole

be real for myself. I choose truth over performance. Peace over pretending.

Wholeness over survival.

Because surviving is not the goal anymore, "thriving" is.

Psychology shows that when a woman endures prolonged stress and instability, her body adapts to survival mode, often without her even realizing it until she's completely exhausted. Mentally, emotionally, and physically. She stays alert, tense, and guarded, always bracing for the next disruption.

Even in calm moments, relaxation feels foreign, unsafe. Not because she's dramatic or too sensitive, but because her nervous system has forgotten what true safety feels like.

Years of disappointment. Years of bearing burdens alone. Years of smiling while shattered inside. It changes you. You stop trusting quiet days. You question consistency. Kindness makes

# My Pain, My Power

## My Pain, My Story, My Journey…My Life

*Living with intention, love and accountability.*

*By Ericka McDole*

you wary because you've learned that love often comes with strings, silence means punishment, and peace can shatter without warning.

So no, she isn't "moody" or "too much." She isn't overreacting. Her body is stuck in fight-or-flight. Her heart is weary. Her spirit is exhausted from years of self-protection to the point where being held truly held, without fear, feels like a distant memory.

If you want to love a woman like this? Be safe. Be steady. Be soft. Don't give her more reasons to question her worth. Don't punish her for needing comfort. Don't make her believe her pain makes her unlovable.

She does not need perfection, she needs patience.

Healing does not begin when life gets quiet. It begins when life stays safe. And too many women are still waiting for that safety to arrive.

# My Pain, My Power

### *My Pain, My Story, My Journey...My Life*

*Living with intention, love and accountability.*

By Ericka McDole

So, I write this chapter for her, the woman still surviving, still searching for peace in the wreckage.

I want you to know: Your power isn't something you earn, it's something you remember.

You were always powerful. Life just made you forget.

But now, now is the time you remember. You rise. You rebuild. You reclaim.

Your name. Your voice. Your joy. Your peace. Your story. Your power "now."

**"My power isn't loud, it doesn't have to be, it's steady. It's in my peace that they tried to take, the boundaries I rebuilt, the access I revoked. It's in my no, loud, proud and final. That's more than survival, that is liberation."**

# My Pain, My Power

*My Pain, My Story, My Journey...My Life*

Living with intention, love and accountability.

By Ericka McDole

### Power Now

It wasn't the scream that saved me,
it was the breath I chose instead.
The way I stood in quiet defiance
when the world expected me to beg.
It wasn't in the fight or fury,
but in the softness, I reclaimed.
In the moment I stopped explaining,
and simply whispered my name.
Power didn't roar, it rose.
Slowly. Gently. On tired legs.
It showed up when I stopped performing
and let my truth break through the eggshells.
I've lived with alarms in my chest,
learned to read danger in peace.
Smiled through storms, trusted no calm,
because safety always had a lease.
But now, I'm choosing different.
I'm choosing "me", without the mask.
Not to prove I'm strong or worthy,

# My Pain, My Power

## *My Pain, My Story, My Journey...My Life*

*Living with intention, love and accountability.*

*By Ericka McDole*

just to feel whole, at last.
My nervous system is learning,
that love doesn't have to wound.
That I can rest without bracing,
and bloom without being pruned.
So, if you call me powerful,
say it with reverence, not fear.
Because my strength was not loud, it was sacred.
And it brought me right here.
This is not survival.
This is not pretend.
This is power, "now. "
And I'll never shrink again.

# My Pain, My Power

## My Pain, My Story, My Journey...My Life

Living with intention, love and accountability.

By Ericka McDole

### Chapter 11: Love Wins in the End

There are some stories that do not get their healing in the middle, they get it in the return.

This chapter is about love. Not the fairy tale kind. Not the love that's always pretty or easy or predictable. But the kind of love that endures after the storm. The kind that survives betrayal, pain, and the silence in between. The kind that grows, not in perfection, but in commitment to keep trying.

I've made peace with the ghosts of my past, those who hurt me, those who failed to protect me, and those who couldn't love me the way I needed. Forgiveness did not come easy. It came in layers, in therapy sessions, in conversations I never thought I would have. But I forgave, not to excuse their behavior, but to free myself from the grip of resentment.

And **I forgave my husband.**

# My Pain, My Power

## *My Pain, My Story, My Journey...My Life*

*Living with intention, love and accountability.*

*By Ericka McDole*

That forgiveness was not automatic. It was hard-earned. He had to face his own demons. He

had to see the damage he caused, not just to our marriage, but to the woman who had stood beside him through every season. He had to show up differently. Not with empty words, but with consistent actions, sincere apologies, and a willingness to be accountable.

**And he did.**

Today, we share a partnership rooted in emotional safety. I finally feel seen. I finally feel protected. Not just physically, but emotionally. He listens now. He checks in. He

acknowledges my pain, not as an inconvenience, but as something sacred that shaped the woman he loves.

He is no longer just the man I married, he's the man I fought to believe he could be. And he fought too. He looked inward. He healed parts of himself he never dared to face. And that healing

# My Pain, My Power

## *My Pain, My Story, My Journey...My Life*

*Living with intention, love and accountability.*

*By Ericka McDole*

made space for our love to become real again, not perfect, but present. To love again after betrayal is a courageous thing. To trust again after devastation is a miracle. We both had to die to the old versions of ourselves to birth something new. Something honest. Something whole.

To the reader: If you've ever thought love couldn't survive what broke you, know this.

Sometimes the breakthrough comes "after" the breakdown. Sometimes reconciliation isn't about returning to what was but redefining what can be.

This chapter is my heart laid bare. It is proof that healing makes room for love. That when both people are willing to grow, to do the work, and to take responsibility, love can win.

It did for me.  Love always wins in the end.

# My Pain, My Power

## *My Pain, My Story, My Journey...My Life*

Living with intention, love and accountability.

By Ericka McDole

### Love Wins in the End

In the ashes of what nearly broke us,

Love rose, not as a whisper, but as a vow.

Not the fairytale, not the fantasy,

But the kind that fights through the fire and stays.

He was broken, and so was I,

But somehow our pieces still reached for one another.

Where silence once sat between us,

Now grace sits at the table.

I am his backbone, the strength he leaned on

When his own knees buckled beneath the

weight of regret.

# My Pain, My Power

## *My Pain, My Story, My Journey...My Life*

*Living with intention, love and accountability.*

*By Ericka McDole*

And he, mine, the steady hand when my soul trembled,

The one who finally learned to catch what he once dropped.

We rebuilt not from memory,

But from honesty.

From the late-night talks and the early-morning apologies.

From faith stitched into the scars we no longer hide.

This love is no longer a performance.

It is a choice, daily made,

To stand beside the same person

With a new heart.

I am the matriarch, warrior in spirit, soft in soul,

# My Pain, My Power

*My Pain, My Story, My Journey...My Life*

Living with intention, love and accountability.

By Ericka McDole

**Fierce protector of my bloodline and my peace.**

**No chaos, no shadow, no outsider's war**

**Will ever undo what I hold sacred.**

**Let them try.**

**I will wrap my arms around my family,**

**And remind them: we don't break here.**

**We bend. We stretch. We rise.**

**Our love is not fragile, it's fortified.**

**By every prayer I whispered into the dark.**

**By every tear that baptized my healing.**

**By every time we chose to stay.**

**Love wins, not because it's easy,**

**But because we worked for it.**

**Fell apart for it.**

# My Pain, My Power

*My Pain, My Story, My Journey...My Life*

Living with intention, love and accountability.

By Ericka McDole

**Found ourselves within it.**

**And when I look at him now, my husband, my friend.**

**I see not just what we lost,**

**But everything we have reclaimed.**

**Love did not just return.**

**It came back transformed.**

**And it won.**

# My Pain, My Power

## *My Pain, My Story, My Journey...My Life*

*Living with intention, love and accountability.*

*By Ericka McDole*

# My Pain, My Power

## *My Pain, My Story, My Journey...My Life*

*Living with intention, love and accountability.*

*By Ericka McDole*

### Final Prayer

*God, I thank You for the strength I did not know I had until I needed it. Thank You for*

*walking with me through the darkest valleys, for holding me close even when I let*

*go, and for never abandoning me when I felt most alone. You were there steady,*

*faithful, unshaken.*

*Lord, I pray for every woman who reads these words. Let her feel Your presence in*

*her stillness and Your power in her pain. Let her hear Your voice louder than her*

*fear and know her worth beyond the wounds she carries. Remind her that broken.*

*does not mean beyond repair, and bruised does not mean beaten. Healing is not just. possible, it is promised. Cover her with grace,*

# My Pain, My Power

## *My Pain, My Story, My Journey...My Life*

*Living with intention, love and accountability.*

*By Ericka McDole*

*Lord. Fill her heart with peace. Give her divine purpose like*

*never before. Let her rise from her pain with dignity, with clarity, and with an*

*unshakable sense of who she is in You.*

*And thank You, God, for not allowing what was meant to break me to succeed. Thank*

*You for turning my breaking point into my breakthrough. I am no longer broken, I*

*am stronger. No longer lost, I am found. No longer silent, I am whole.*

*Thank You for not letting the enemy destroy what You put together. Continue to*

*surround me and those I love with Your shield of protection, Your endless mercy,*

*and Your unfailing grace.*

*In Jesus' name, Amen.*

# My Pain, My Power

## *My Pain, My Story, My Journey...My Life*

*Living with intention, love and accountability.*

*By Ericka McDole*

### Epilogue

This journey was never about perfection, it was about truth.

Each chapter has been a reckoning, a healing, a reclamation. These words were born from nights I couldn't sleep, from days I could barely breathe, and from moments when I almost gave up on myself. But I didn't. I kept showing up. Broken, bleeding, but still breathing.

To every woman who has ever questioned her worth, who's been betrayed, silenced, or overlooked I see you. I was you. And maybe in some ways, I still am. But now, I carry wisdom where wounds once lived. I carry grace where guilt once sat. I carry power where shame used to whisper.

This book is not the end of my story, it's the

# My Pain, My Power

## *My Pain, My Story, My Journey...My Life*

*Living with intention, love and accountability.*

*By Ericka McDole*

beginning of my freedom.

Forgiveness saved me.
Faith grounded me.
Love, real, raw, accountable love, healed me.

To my past: Thank you for the lessons.
To my pain: Thank you for the growth.
To my future: I'm coming, whole and unafraid.

May every reader close this book feeling seen, heard, and inspired to rise. And when life threatens to break you, may you remember:

You are not what happened to you. You are what you choose to become.

This is my legacy.
This is my peace.
This is my power.
– Ericka

# My Pain, My Power

***My Pain, My Story, My Journey…My Life***

*Living with intention, love and accountability.*

*By Ericka McDole*

Thank you

Made in the USA
Coppell, TX
11 January 2026

68848015R00056